THE 5 KEYS

SUCCESSFUL

AND

LASTING MARRIAGE

Simple Secrets To A Healthy, Happy, Outstanding, Enjoyable, And Thriving Marriage

ROBERT D. GOTMAN, MD

DEDICATION

To the love of my life Jena, the wife of my youth, for her commitment to making our marriage work. Thank you for choosing to take this journey with me. I love you so much and I will choose you over again.

And to our lovely kids for their support and sacrifice.

Robert D. Gotman, MD

TABLE OF CONTENT

INTRODUCTION

Success in marriage doesn't come just by meeting the right person but by being the right mate.

Years prior, my family and I accepted a moderate way of life. We concluded that an excessive amount of messiness had gathered in our home and it was requesting a lot of our cash, energy, and valuable time.

We set out on an excursion to sell, give, reuse, or eliminate however many of the insignificant belongings from our home as could be allowed. It was indeed the best decision we ever made towards having a successful marriage relationship.

As soon as we started eliminating the "stuff" from our life, we saw an overall new world open up. We suddenly realized we had more energy for the things that mattered most.

Presently, accordingly, we invest more energy during dinner, we go for long strolls as a family, and we have had the option to set aside cash for some, worthwhile experiences like an end of the week at the beachside, for instance.

Eliminating the superfluous items has permitted us to zero in additional on the fundamentals. What's more, we have found that genuine life is found there.

Often, our relationships follow a similar direction.

Right away, when we have only one another, we center eagerly around the important building blocks of a healthy and successful marriage. However, as our relationship moves ahead, "stuff" begins to gather and starts to take away our attention from the actual basics of what makes a healthy marriage.

suddenly, we stress more over the appraisal of the worth of our home than the worth of our relationship. We check the strength of our retirement account more frequently than the state of our marriage. Or then again we invest more energy dealing with the car in the carport than the other individual in our bed.

Certain things begin to creep into our homes and lives and before long begin to place a demand on our money, energy, and valuable time. Thus, we have little left over for really focusing on the actual components of a successful marriage.

Clever couples are aware that a nice house, vehicle, or retirement plan might seem good to have, however they don't make a happy and successful marriage. They understand that there are undeniably more important principles affecting everything.

They have figured out how to put away their cash, energy, and time into the 5 keys to a healthy, happy, lasting, and successful marriage:

As shown by studies, consistent, little, and simple changes create a successful marriage. Beneath, this book outlines the five keys to a healthy, happy, and successful marriage, and gives useful ideas that couples can carry out at the present moment. These tips are crucial for anybody in a relationship, regardless of whether or not you are a newlywed or allude to yourselves as old Ball 'n' Chain, or intending to walk down the aisle.

CHAPTER ONE
EXPECT LESS AND GET MORE FROM YOUR PARTNER

S adly, we are raised to believe in fairytale endings and we might take a few bogus viewpoints on reality with us into adulthood. We must realize that, while marriage can be something excellent, it isn't easy, nor will it at any point be perfect.

Have sensible assumptions, be realistic, and don't succumb to fantasy - you might come to realize you were horribly disillusioned. This isn't just probably the best element of a successful marriage, however, plays an important part in your joy as an individual as well.

Nobody is without a fault. You should acknowledge the great with the awful defects whatnot. There is a degree of effortlessness required-understanding that they are human and will commit errors. What's more, you should likewise recognize what you're good at and figure out how to balance each other. One of you might be better at dealing with the cash the other might be better at dealing with the children's bustling timetables. Figure out how to use your strength as a benefit. Simultaneously, figure out how to recognize your shortcoming and attempt to further develop them. It's vital to comprehend your companion's shortcomings and figure out how to offset them with your strength. Acknowledge them for what and who they are and allow them to grow and develop over time.

The key to a healthy and successful marriage lies in understanding this straightaway. While asking or convincing your partner, you are just zeroing in on his/her shortcomings or issues. Alter your viewpoint promptly and begin zeroing in on certain qualities all things being equal.

Many individuals accept that contention is a kryptonite to relationships. However, it's really frustration, in particular, dissatisfaction, as a result of a partner's unmet expectations.

Happy couples have pragmatic expectations, both with regards to relationships overall and about their relationship specifically. For example, one of the couple's myths is that happy couples don't have disagreements or conflicts. Conflicts or disagreements are inescapable. Truth be told, on the off chance that you're not having conflicts, you're not discussing the significant issues in your relationship.

PRACTICAL TIP: You and your partner should independently write your best two expectations for your relationship (i.e., how you would want your partner to treat you; your major issues). This basic action permits couples to see what's essential to one another. In the event that your partner doesn't know about your needs and expectations, how would they meet them?

Robert D. Gotman, MD

CHAPTER TWO
GIVE MOTIVATIONS AND PRIZES

Underestimating each other might be the most poisonous element of all. When they are agreeable and comfortable, it is easy for couples to start to slip into a smug state, where they begin to take each other for granted and at this point, expectations will begin to form.

This is just an issue of human instinct, as we become familiar with what is natural, yet in marriage, you totally should never come to where you underestimate your partner or take him/her for granted.

Promise to regard your partner endlessly regardless. Keep away from suppositions, and propose to do decent things for your partner whenever the situation allows. Best relationships have partners who attest to this.

One of the ways of doing this is through powerful assertion. This is vital to a healthy and successful marriage. An emotional assertion is telling your partner that they're exceptional, esteemed and you don't underestimate them.

Couples show emotional certification through words and activities. It's just about as basic as saying 'I love you' or 'You're my dearest companion.' Certifiable practices can be anything from turning the espresso pot on toward the beginning of the day for your partner to sending them a hot email to filling their tank with gas.

A commendation daily they say fends the separation lawyer off. Recognizing your partner's positive attributes each day, and offering praises will go quite far in your relationship.

Remain positive, and monitor as your companion progresses nicely. When it becomes tough in your relationship and your partner begins to show those negative attributes, rather than zeroing in on them, have a go at shifting gears, and pointing out the positive things instead.

As opposed to prevalent thinking, research has shown that men need more emotional insistence than ladies since ladies can get it from others in their lives.

The key is to be consistent rather than loads of it at once.

PRACTICAL TIP: A nice word daily can keep a couple happy and guarantee their marriage is successful. Work on saying something nice to your partner or doing something special for them each day.

Robert D. Gotman, MD

CHAPTER THREE
HAVE DAY-BY-DAY BRIEFINGS FOR FURTHER DEVELOPED COMMUNICATION

Most couples will say that they impart. Be that as it may, this communication is normally the thing is known as keeping up with the family, which incorporates discusses taking care of the bills, purchasing food, assisting the children with schoolwork, or calling the parents-in-law.

We really need to talk.

Most partners fear this sentence however do you have any idea about that on the off chance that you are considering how to have an effective relationship, making a stage for solid discussions is the best approach?

While all ladies should work in the specialty of undivided attention, I especially accentuate this as an area of extraordinary consideration for men. Time and again, men don't understand that all their partners' needs from them are a listening ear. This is because of their programming and how they are educated to connect with others.

You need to understand there's a huge difference between listening and hearing. Listening includes our hearts. hence, need to learn the act of listening with your ears but hearing with your heart. You can't simply hear what they say, however you need to get what they mean. For instance 'You're never at home' may just simply mean 'I miss you and I want to get to spend quality with you.' Presently hopefully they will simply SAY THAT! Yet, we as a whole realize that this isn't dependably the situation.

Effective listening is an important key to a successful marriage for that matter, and even to every other kind of relationship.

Significant communication implies getting to know your partner's internal world. Whenever you're truly cheerful, you realize what really matters to your partner and get them.

It is not always easy for somebody to truly discover the intentions of another person. So the following are some interesting points to consider:

The manner of speaking is vital, speaking loudly implies they are sincerely attempting to convey an idea there are extraordinary feelings behind what they said, it might even come with the eventual result of being impolite

- Observe non-verbal communication of moving eyes, grinning, crossed arms, and so forth
- Figure out how to be decisive express what you feel without being forceful (attempting to cause them to hear you) or being excessively detached (not having any desire to offend them).
- Be clear, brief, and direct.
- Figure out how to work it out. Take a seat at the kitchen table and talk about the accounts, the

children, and retirement-whatever is essential to your relationship.

- Be conscious don't talk over them or cause them to feel as you couldn't care less. Moreso, regardless of whether you care, make an effort to help them by saying such things like 'wow,' 'sorry, you feel as such' 'that must truly be hard' or 'I get what you are talking about.

- Realize that your sentiments matter to express what you feel and attempt to track down a center ground (compromise)

- Effectively stand by listening to what they need to say and request an explanation on the off chance that you don't comprehend DON'T Expect us as a whole to know what that implies!

PRACTICAL TIP: Practice the 10-minute rule. That includes every day conversing with your partner for somewhere around 10 minutes about some different options from the following four themes: work, family, who will do what around the house, or your relationship.

Couples can talk via telephone, by email, or face to face. The key is to get to know your partner.

Not certain what to inquire? Attempt these example themes: What have you been most pleased with this year? On the off chance that you scored that sweepstake, where might you need to venture out to and why? For sure are your best five motion pictures ever?

Robert D. Gotman, MD

CHAPTER FOUR
EXECUTE CHANGE

E ach marriage eventually gets into a trench. Executing change can help get it out of there, and there are numerous ways of doing that. One method for executing change is to add a new thing or unexpectedly do something old differently. The primary thought is to mirror your relationship when you initially met each other.

You have to find out imaginative ways of keeping up with newness in your relationship. ensure you make yourself appealing and attractive to your partner. There should be some degree of intimacy for your marriage to be successful. and it does not have to do with just sex but on a more intimate level. Zero in on what you love about them-the things that attracted you to them at the outset. Likewise, consider the things that you have come to love about them along the way. You must desire your

Partner for their inward beauty as well as outward. Ensure you do not depend on outward appearance to keep you in love, however, look for qualities about them that make you need them more. Zero in on your intimacy and increased closeness through communication and emotional ties.

Always remember the things that brought you together and realize that marriage is certainly not a two-way road. It is one way you both decide to walk in it together-both similarly liable for where it takes your family. Choose to make the journey together and be inseparable.

PRACTICAL TIP: To lessen boredom and keep things fresh, change up your daily schedule. For example, Rather than going to a similar eatery, discover some new outlandish café in the city. Excursion someplace new or take a class together.

Another system is to do an excitement-creating movement or [an action that] provides you with a flood of adrenal or fervor. How we find is that assuming you treat movement with your partner, the excitement or adrenaline created by that other action can really get moved to your spouse or relationship.

Practice together, ride a thrill ride or see an unnerving film.

Robert D. Gotman, MD

CHAPTER FIVE
MINIMIZE COST AND KEEP ADVANTAGES HIGH

In light of recent research, happy couples practice a 5 to 1 proportion. That is, they have five good sentiments or experiences to each one gloomy inclination or experience.

This does not in any way suggest you have to approach your relationship with a calculator. In any case, it's critical to review your relationship routinely and think about the costs and benefits.

Many couples accept that there should be a harmony between the advantages and disadvantages, yet studies have shown the accompanying portrayal: Assuming you have the positives in your right hand and the cost/negative practices in your left hand, ensure your right goes way down, so The positive things truly need to offset the negatives.

One of the ways of keeping up with the 5: 1 proportion of advantages to cost is to guarantee that for each criticism that makes a withdrawal from the relationship, you should put aside five installments of positive articulations or experiences to simply return to where you began.

PRACTICAL TIP: You can review your relationship by basically making a conventional advantages and disadvantages list. Take a piece of paper, and share it into two halves. On the right side, record every one of the positive feelings and practices associated with your partner and relationship. On the left side, write down every negative thing you don't like about your partner and relationship. Once more, Ensure the right side is in every case significantly longer than the left side. Request that your partner does this, as well.

CHAPTER SIX
CONCLUSION

By and large, happy couples give attention to the positives of their relationship. So it's essential to fortify what's now working on the positives, this increases a couple's capacity to manage the adverse issues in their relationship.

If you deal with your marriage like a two-way road, you must understand that you are going in a different direction with your partner. To be successful, you and your spouse should be on a one-way adventure! We found, rather than give as one gets, couples should work at their relationship together. After a few experiments, we came to realize the solution to any decision driving a critical change in our family's future was to talk about our desires and decide the bearing we needed our family to take. We persistently ask one another on the off chance that we are content with the manner in which we are raising our kids, with how we treat one another, and some other part of where our family has been or where we are going. Marriage is certainly not a two-way road; it is a one-way we decided to walk down the road of our marriage together. We are both responsible for where the road takes our family and we have seen this decision pay off in ways we could have never imagined.

Now it's your turn to begin the journey with your partner towards making your marriage a healthy, happy, and successful one. If Jena and I could do it, you too can!